# Mind of an Artist (Poetry & Art)

Jo Ann Atcheson Gray, Anna Elizabeth

# Contents

# *Words From An Artist*

Words From An Artist


Art can be an enjoyable passion. No talent or professionalism, only what makes you happy!

Grab a canvas, a journal, poetry, or anything that you can express your fantasy or passion and create your masterpieces!

Hope you enjoy my little book of art and poetry!

May it inspire everyone to express their hidden desires and fantasies within this vast reality!!


JO ANN


"Who says your fantasies can't collide with your reality?"

"Art can be such a beautiful profession."

"Lust. Such a small word with so much meaning attached to it."

Jo Ann

# Poem 1: Walking Away

**W**alking Away

The sadness lingers mentally
Decision must be made.
Should one stay or eventually
Should one go, never to be repaid?

Fate can be cruel to one
Destiny, leaving you undone.
Reality turns from fantasy
As walking away has won.

# Poem 2: Love Dies

L ove Dies

Darkness creeps in.
Night.
Silence is deafening.
Love Ends.
Shadows start to stir.
Heart ceases to feel.
Love Ends.
Eternity awaits.
Darkness creeps in.
Love ends.

# Poem 3: Blood of a Vampire

B lood of a Vampire

Blood runs cold as ice within my veins
Flowing like a river, never to drain.
Never to love, never to feel.
Eternity for one such as I is real.

Loneliness within this vastness
Closes my eyes to my reality.
As this blood runs through with fastness.
Finding the blood of a vampire
Isn't just formality.

# Poem 4: Eternity

E ternity

Never dying, never crying
Feeling a vast loneliness
Longing for peace while trying
To fill my undead heart with happiness.

Eternity is such a cruel word
To walk this earth alone
Never ceasing of things heard
As I continue into the unknown.

# Poem 5: Darkness

D arkness

No sight. Mere blackness.
Feeling alone and shattered
Within this vastness.
Darkness all but tattered
As one's life doesn't seem to matter.

# Poem 6: Into My Eyes

I nto My Eyes

Shadows peer unseen to one's desire
Glimpse of darkness, light to my fire
Into my eyes, stories untold
Of dangers that are ages old
Sadness deems around all corners
As flashes of light become
Such a border
Into my eyes, you'll get lost
Blinded by pain that wasn't
A total loss.

# Poem 7: Blood

# Sacrifice

B lood Sacrifice

Dark moon rises, gray clouds thicken
A dagger taken, the blood revealed
Weakness begins to quicken
Sealing the bloody, vicious deal.

Heartbeat ceases to beat
As darkness shadows over reality
No more feeling, no more heat
The coldness sets in to one's insanity.

# Poem 8: A Vampire's Seduction

A Vampire's Seduction

Her kiss is cold upon my lips
As my body warms my blood
Her touch is ice upon my hips
As desire comes in like a flood.

Her fangs pierce my neck
As my pain is only brief
The blood flows out like a wreck
As my body weakens as a thief.

Darkness falls all around
As life is slowing draining
Feeling no longer abounds

As my blood is never refraining.

# Poem 9: Lady

L ady

The lady closes her eyes to
What is seen
Her need to rise is far from
In between
Blessings fly away within
The clouds
As she screams for love
Entirely too loud
Eternity is all that lies
In the distance
If only it could really
Exist in an instant
Darkness closes into one's
Own heart
As she expresses her pain

Through such art.

# Poem 10: Red Rose

R ed Rose

Take this rose, red as fire
Drop it to the soil, my deepest desire
Lying in darkness, voices I only hear
Saying good-byes as I shed a tear.

Left alone within this silence
Only this red rose I hold as guidance
Closing my eyes, I know it's real
Death appears to come, no matter the deal.

Drifting into the vast unknown
No shadows around to call my own
Knowing this fate, I cannot heal
As I hold this red rose, I no longer feel.

# Poem 11: The Heart

The Heart

Ask me how I knew.
Ask me how I know.
Ask me when we're through
And I will tell you no.

# Poem 12: Fearful Immortal

Fearful Immortal

Your eyes are hollow

Your pain is deep

Blood flows in your veins

Yet its color you cannot keep

Darkness is your light

Yet it holds your heart tight

Eternity is far away

For one such affright.

# Poem 13: A Vampire's Tear

A Vampire's Tear

Blood drips from my eye,
The pain ceases from my heart.
I no longer feel,
I only express through art.
This blood tear falls from my cheek
As I throw this canvas into the creek.
Memories to bury, to drown,
Never again to resurface the pain I unbound.
A blood tear falls once more
As I let go, accepting it nevermore.

# Poem 14: The Perfect Funeral

T he Perfect Funeral

Red roses strolled all around
As I lay in my pearl coffin silently
Tears of sadness abound
As words are spoken perfectly.
White satin dress covers my body
As I hear dirt thrown vaguely
The music stops, silence is hardy
Darkness that tells me, it's gravely.
A red rose I hold near my chest
No light to see the thorn.
I close my eyes as if to rest
No feeling, only numb, I am torn.

# Poem 15: Angel's Wings

A ngel's Wings

Wings so fierce, so wide, open
For only a few to see
Heavenly bliss to share
Never to flee
Protects you through the
Darkest of nights
Always prepared for whatever
The fight
Shields one from the
Dimmest of light
Until one is prepared
For such a flight.

# Poem 16: Candle

C andle

Flame burning bright as the sun
Flickering as the wax runs slow
Darkness surrounds the fun
As the candle gets too low.

Barely a hint of light
As the night takes control
Candle deems 'good night'
As the flame is no more bold.

# Poem 17: The Vampire's Kiss

T he Vampire's Kiss

Quietly. Cold. Seduction takes hold.

Lost in the vastness of secrets untold.

His kiss, his eternal lust

Closes my eyes, leaving nothing but dust.


Taste of blood, a bitter delight

As darkness fades away the light.

Lost in this numbness, so faint.

This kiss, this vampire, isn't a saint.


The warm blood painful upon my lips

As the vampire takes his final sip.

No more reality, all is unknown

For all eternity is unnaturally shown.

# Poem 18: Magic For Love

## M agic For Love

Shimmers of light, with crystals so bright

Sparkles of tears, joy just in sight.

Pinprick of blood from a fingertip

That can only be tasted once upon the lip.

Dash of a crow's feather, so black

Puff of smoke to simmer the pack.

A virgin's blood to seal the deal

To make this magic seem so real.

Soft words spoken in a trance

With a witch's eyelash to have a chance.

The magic is complete, pure perfection

For love to show in a magical projection.

Magical love to show the way

To the heart, who has gone astray
Breathe easy, the task is done
Affection and desire have already won.

# Poem 19: Mystic Gem

M ystic Gem

A gem so bright, so magical

Holds the power inside

Red as a ruby, it couldn't be practical

A curse that will not hide.

The heart strives for peace

As the gem holds no release

Only love can place the crack

With the gem not holding back.

Power of decision to be made

To break the gem by love

A choice from a broken heart stayed

Only the power coming from above.

A gem no longer withheld

For love can conquer all

Leaving the crack impaled

With the heart never again behind a wall.

# Poem 20: Undone

U ndone

The vastness.
Can't be undone.
The sacredness.
Will leave you undone.
Loneliness.
Everyone is undone.
The hurtfulness.
The heart is undone.
Spirituality.
The soul is undone.
Reality. Fantasy.
Is never undone.

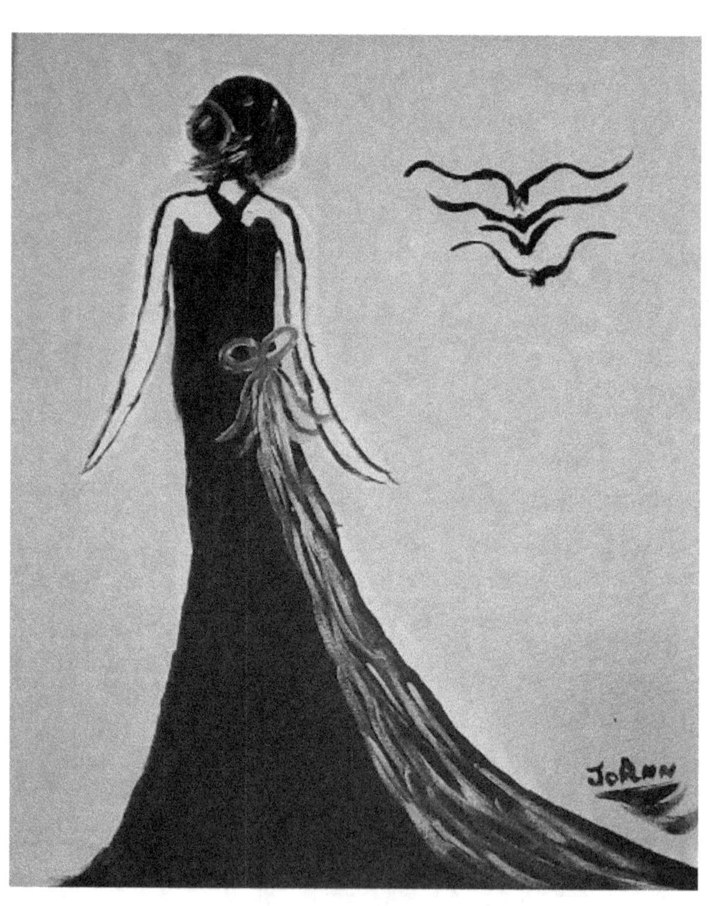

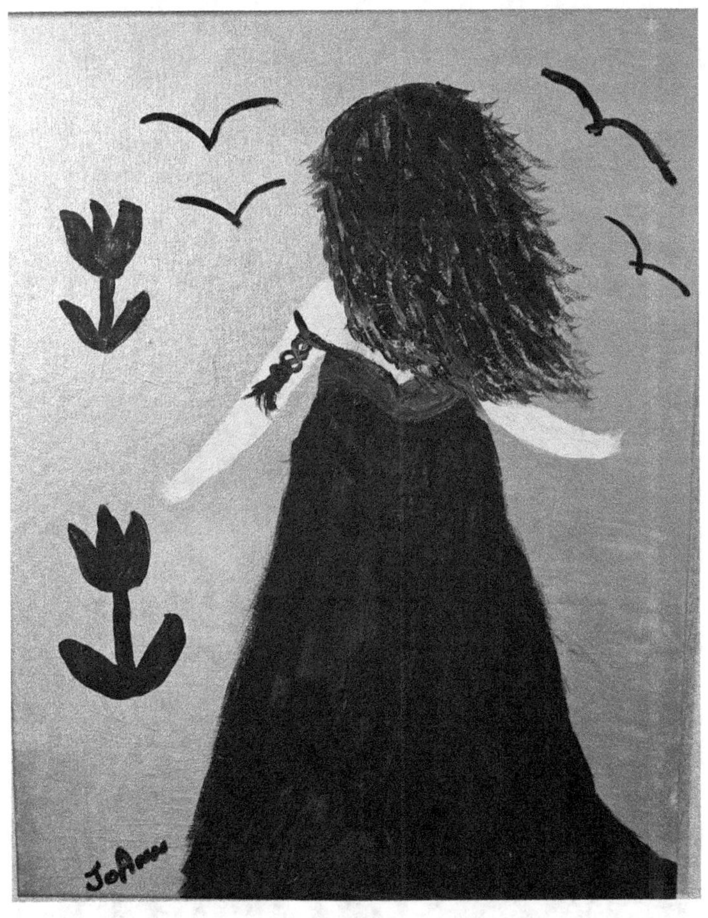

JoAnn

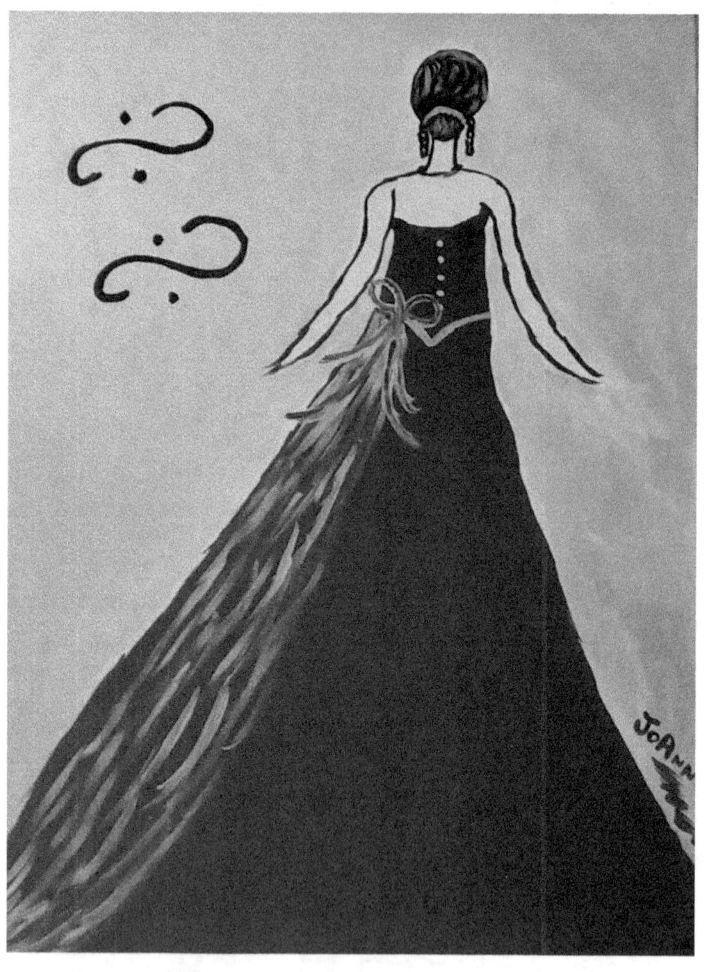

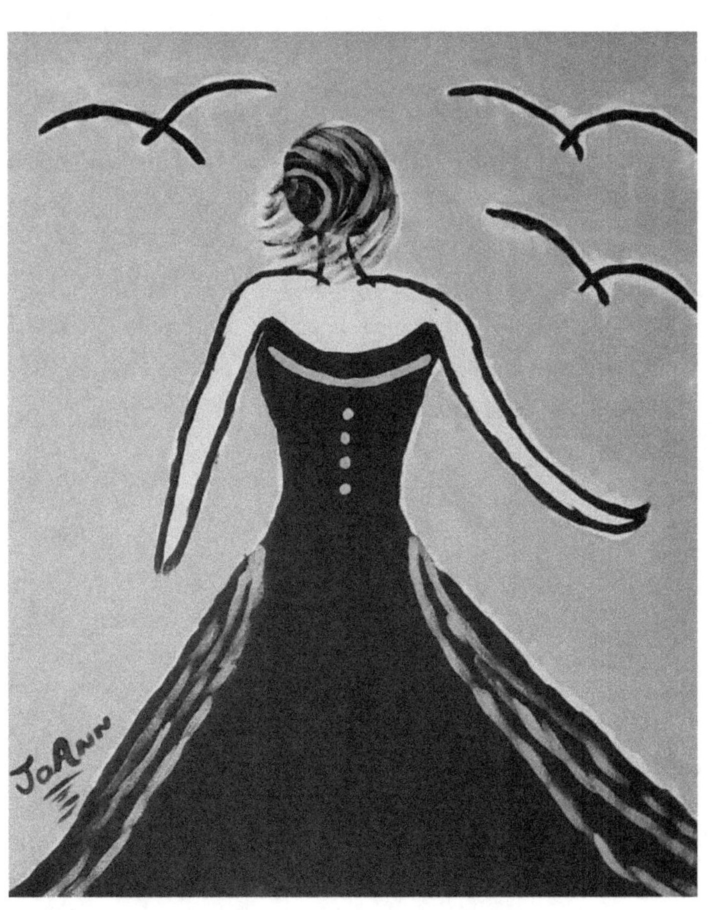

# Thank You!

Thank You so much!

Hope you enjoyed my small poetry book!

Jo Ann